A CHILDREN'S BOOK OF INSECTS FROM ANT TO ZEBRA CATERPILLAR

BY GARRY DEGROOD

Dedicated to Cindy, who restores my faith in the natural order.

"Love is all-encompassing, as natural as it is pure." (Anonymous)

A CHILDREN'S BOOK OF INSECTS FROM A-Z is an introduction to the study of insects or entomology. It is intended for young children and it is based on the same principles as the Dr. Seuss series of books. The use of imaginative rhyme, illustrations, and repetition is a proven methodology for learning vocabulary. I utilize rhyme and illustrations as a means of capturing a child's imagination and hopefully stimulating a curiosity about the world of insects. I use both simple and sophisticated rhymes because it is my contention that children are capable of much more than we give them credit for. Some of the words used will undoubtedly prove to be unfamiliar and will require an explanation. As a parent, reading along with a child is one of life's simple pleasures. It is my hope that parents will enjoy this book as much as the children. It was my intention to inject a touch of humor into the subject matter. This book is better suited for young children who already possess a good, basic vocabulary. I hope that their thirst for knowledge will engender a lifetime of interest in science and nature.

THE **A**NT

Don't you laugh at me!

I'm part of a colony.

And don't you think me weak.

Judge me by my physique.

My legs may be long and thin.

But I have mandibles on my chin.

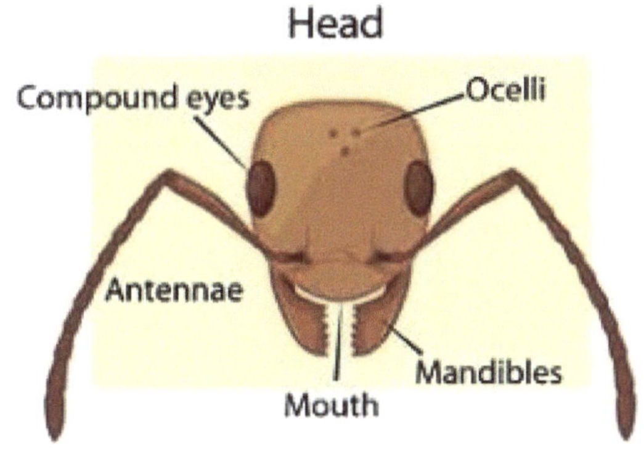

I am less than a half-inch long,

Nevertheless, I'm incredibly strong.

I can lift eight times my weight.

In comparison to me, how do you rate?

I dig tunnels, I'm a natural miner.

A dedicated worker, there's nobody finer.

Like the honey bees, we have a queen.

But she's far too busy, rarely seen.

She is bigger than the rest of us.

We depend on her, she's worth the fuss.

THE (HONEY) Bee

I'm as busy as can be.

I'm a hard-working honey bee.

As I fly around,

I make a buzzing sound.

As I fly my heart sings,

To the rhythm of my wings.

I fly from flower to flower.

Nature's beauty provides the power.

Into the center I will dive.

Carry the treasure to the hive.

In the hive, we'll turn nectar into honey.

It's serious work, nothing funny.

We'll save the honey for a rainy day.

But beekeepers always seem to take it away.

We will have to start all over again.

Working even harder because of the beekeeper men.

The honey is stored in wax honeycombs.

Cells which double as bee larvae homes.

While we all serve the queen,

I'll show the workers where I've been.

So I'll do a little dance.

Hold them spellbound, in a trance.

round dance

waggle dance

Reveal the proper vector.

To find the sweetest nectar.

I wish this rhyme had a happy ending.

I'm not sure, on you I'm depending.

Scores of us each year are dying.

The problem is serious, I'm not lying.

I am sad to say that our future's in doubt.

I won't brag but my importance I'll tout.

If it were not for me.

There'd be far less food you see.

Flowering plants and trees need me to thrive.

So it's extremely important that I survive.

THE COCKROACH

I've been around since the dawn of man.

I know that you're not my biggest fan.

I like to live where conditions are right.

I thrive on squalor and urban blight.

Just try to get rid of me, once I get in!

I'll settle down, invite all my kin.

A cockroach can multiply extremely fast.

We can survive a nuclear blast!

During daylight hours we rarely appear.

Just you wait until nighttime draws near!

All through your house, we'll start to roam.

We'll make ourselves comfortable, call this our home.

Should you get up and turn on the light.

You'll be greeted by a horrible sight.

Thousands of incredibly fast-moving roaches.

Disappearing in an instant as a human approaches.

THE DRAGONFLY

I've been around since the dinosaur.

I'm a hungry predator, I always want more.

I can eat my weight in mosquitoes each day.

Rely on me, I'll make them pay.

Four large wings on my back and a long, slender tail.

Mosquitoes try to escape, but to no avail.

My body and wings shine in a rainbow of colors.

I'm unique among insects, not like the others.

I am an insect which does the world good.

Please protect me, just like you should.

THE EARWIG

I am an earwig, but let's make this clear.

It's a myth that I like to live in your ear.

I'm sure you've heard stories about what I do.

People hate me even though the stories aren't true.

I have forceps at the end of my tail.

If they are curved, it means I'm a male.

I thought females were the ones with the curves.

The excitable ones, all emotions and nerves.

The forceps are used to grab, hold or fight.

The pincers are strong, the grip is tight.

An earwig's diet is plant and insect matter.

An omnivore's task is to grow fatter and fatter.

We are nocturnal, we like the dark.

During the day, we might hide under bark.

To remain unseen, seek some sort of protection.

Hunt for food by night or a mate by selection.

THE FIREFLY

I am a firefly, I glow in the night.

As I fly in the dark, I provide my own light.

The glow will assist us fireflies in mating.

Just think of it as our way of firefly dating.

If you catch me and rub my rear end.

Your fingers will glow, please show a friend.

The glow is phosphorescence, a really long word.

Some call it magic, that's just absurd.

Study insects like me and you will soon see.

Ours is a world of discovery.

People can learn a lot from a bug.

Don't think you're superior, don't be so smug!

Catching Fireflies

THE GRASSHOPPER

I'm glad it soon will be spring.

I'm grateful for the green grass it will bring.

For I have quite an appetite.

As do my friends whom I'll invite.

To dine upon the long, thin blades.

As thick as the Florida Everglades.

They call me names like nuisance or pest.

Because of all the green things I ingest.

Just try to catch me if you can.

For I can jump a lengthy span.

My strong rear legs allow me to hop.

From field to field, crop to crop.

I apologize if I cause you trouble.

Eat your lawn and leave you stubble.

Don't blame me for the damage I do.

I'm not guilty from my point of view.

THE HOUSEFLY

I like to keep warm, perhaps indoors?

Buzz in your ear while you do chores.

I hope you don't swat me, please leave me alone.

I don't appreciate your angry tone.

I'll admit that I land on your food.

Call me a nuisance, call me crude.

Is that any way to treat a guest?

Chase me around, call me a pest.

Sure, I spread germs and bacteria.

Is that any reason for the hysteria?

Why I can even fly upside down!

Cheap entertainment, I'm quite a clown.

Zigging and zagging while you flail away.

Your aim is lousy I dare to say.

Office building, house, apartment (or flat).

Just try to get me, uh oh! Splat!

THE LETTER 'I'

'I' is for insects, the subject of this book.

I'd like to thank you for having a look.

Insects come in all shapes and sizes.

Both good and bad, please don't despise us.

If you insist on a particular sample.

Here is an insect, a perfect example.

The ichneumon wasp begins with an 'I'.

I can't think of another, no matter how hard I try.

THE JAPANESE BEETLE

The Japanese beetle is really quite tiny.

You'll recognize me, my body's quite shiny.

I'm colored iridescent copper and green.

One of the most beautiful beetles you've ever seen.

I come from the land of the rising sun.

As tough as a samurai, if you pardon my pun.

I don't have a sword but leaves I'll slice through.

You can't possibly imagine the damage I do.

I cause damage to all sorts of crops.

Like flowers, fruits, berries, and hops.

The larvae feed on roots while I feed on leaves.

I am one of a farmer's pet peeves.

Japanese beetles can breed very fast.

From east to west our range is vast.

Try to prevent us from further spreading.

Our eggs can be found in most plant-soils (bedding).

Before you take plants across the border.

Remember you can upset the natural order.

THE LETTER 'K'

There are few insects which begin with a 'K'.

So listen to me, hear what I say.

You can be the first kid on your block.

To name a new insect which can crawl, fly or walk.

May I be so bold as to make a suggestion?

Is it large enough to answer my question?

Does the insect look like a king?

If it is so, please name this thing.

King beetle, king fly, you get the picture.

Your discovery will become a permanent fixture.

Of books and journals, all scientific.

People will applaud you, think you're terrific.

If the insect deserves to be crowned a king.

Just think of the attention that it will bring.

In the insect world, there is already a queen.

It's about time to balance the scene.

There's no need for an apology.

There's no sexism in entomology!

THE LADYBUG

I'm red with little black polka dots.

You can find me in leafy spots.

I'm cute, small and my body is round.

I fly and crawl without a sound.

I'm very familiar, you'll know me by sight.

But if I'm bothered, I'll take flight.

I can't fly for very long.

Just enough until I am gone.

I get rid of bugs that are bad.

If you don't believe me, go ask your Dad.

Destructive aphids are a favorite snack.

You understand, you're on the right track.

Ladybugs are known as a sign of spring.

Some people believe good luck I will bring.

THE MOSQUITO

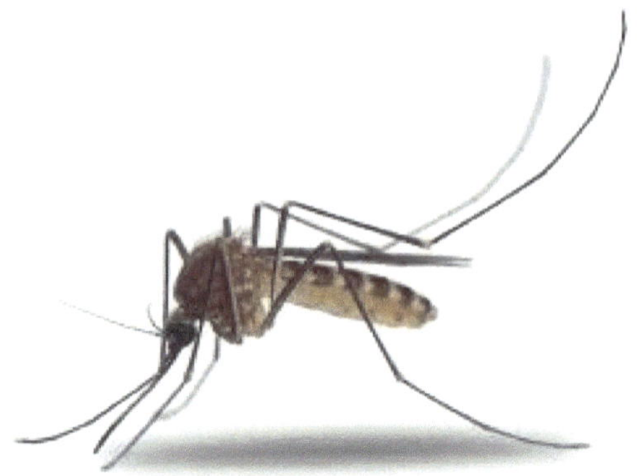

I was around when dinosaurs thrived.

They died out but I survived.

Once I land on you, I can begin.

To drill a hole through your tender skin.

To lay my eggs, I need your blood.

One mosquito can turn into a flood.

Sometimes you won't even feel me bite.

When I've had my fill, I'll take flight.

I'll lay my eggs in stagnant waters.

Soon you'll meet my hungry daughters.

They have the ability to detect your breath.

Mosquitoes bring disease, mosquitoes bring death.

We like to rest during the heat of the day.

When it cools down, we'll come out to play.

Warm-blooded creatures are our favorite prey.

So wear lots of repellant to keep us away.

THE NYMPH

A nymph is an insect young, developed, yet small.

It resembles an adult after all.

Think of a nymph as one of life's stages.

A rite of passage, a teen who ages.

Adulthood is not far away.

Provided the nymph can find a way.

To avoid predators, find the right meal.

A place to hide and appearance conceal.

To settle down and find a mate.

Perpetuate the species, procreate.

A nymph has the whole world ahead.

Young and spry, far from dead.

And like a teen, this stage is brief.

Less than a season, the turn of a leaf.

"So enjoy yourself" to the nymph I'll say.

Carpe diem, seize the day.

THE OLEANDER APHID

I range in color from orange to yellow.

I might be small but I'm a pesky fellow.

I'm the only one in this close-up photo.

Yet I am typical of all aphids in toto.

Where you find one, you'll find many.

Dozens can fit on the head of a penny.

We suck the life right out of plants.

Infest a large area like army ants.

We like to go on long, healthy walks.

Climb up and down tender green stalks.

We feed on milkweed ripened by sun.

But oleander is our favorite one.

This is the reason why we were named.

Oleander aphids and why we are blamed.

THE PRAYING MANTIS

My arms are folded as if in prayer.

As lethal as a vampire slayer.

Motionless, I shall lie in wait.

For something to grab and seal its fate.

Sometimes I'm brown, sometimes I'm green.

I look like a twig to remain unseen.

And when it's time to spring my trap.

My arms snap forward and zap!

Just like that, I've captured my prey.

I will then feed for the rest of the day.

THE QUEEN

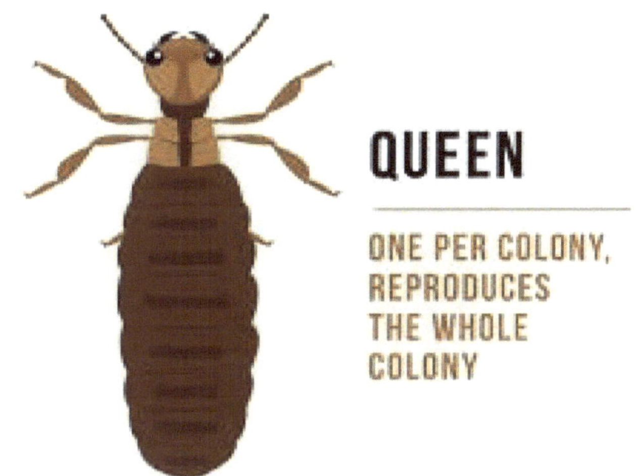

QUEEN

ONE PER COLONY,
REPRODUCES
THE WHOLE
COLONY

Ant, bee, and termite queens are the matriarchs.

We are usually larger or have distinguishing marks.

Though I'm a queen, I don't wear a crown.

Hive or colony, I won't let them down.

I can't do everything when I'm all alone.

I need my workers to retain my throne.

The workers assure that I am well fed.

While I'm worshipped, it won't go to my head.

Queens lay the eggs so our numbers will grow.

Our solemn duty, not a tale of woe.

I have workers attend to me.

Some are in charge of the nursery.

Mound, hive or nest.

A queen has no rest.

THE RHINOCEROS BEETLE

With a long spike on my head, I resemble a rhino.

No cave-dwelling beetle, I'm black, no albino.

Like most beetles, I'm incredibly strong.

Even though I'm only a few inches long.

I may look dangerous, but I'm not a threat.

In some countries I'm even kept as a pet.

In Asia, fights between males are wagered.

It's lucky that we're not endangered.

People call me the heavyweight champ.

Of the beetle world, dry or damp.

There is one opponent who worries me.

A giant among beetles as you can see.

The goliath beetle lives up to its name.

I'd rather not fight him, if it's all the same.

My wings are hidden, they fold right in.

They are a special growth of skin.

It's a miracle that something as big as I.

Can spread stubby wings, take off, and fly.

THE Spider

A spider has legs, the number is eight.

My ravenous appetite I hope to sate.

Almost invisible is the web I weave.

Flying insects I intend to deceive.

The strands of the web are sticky and strong.

I'm very patient, the wait can be long.

I wait near the center to feel a vibration.

When a fly is caught, I can't describe my elation!

I'll hurry to the fly and I'll wrap it up tight.

It'll try to escape, it'll put up a fight.

Sometimes I'll wait and eat it after.

A meal is a source of joy, of laughter.

Some spiders have a poisonous bite.

Is this the reason why people take fright?

Tarantula, Daddy Long Legs, Brown Recluse.

Know all your spiders, there's just no excuse.

A Black Widow has a distinctive hourglass in red.

A reminder that in time, you might end up dead.

While on the subject, I should mention.

If you are bitten by one, seek medical attention.

Spiders are creepy, but most are harmless like me.

There's nothing to be afraid of, don't you agree?

THE TICK

I am known as a parasite.

I need blood, so I must bite.

When I drink, my body will swell.

Wooded areas are where I like to dwell.

I resemble a miniature spider.

As I feed my body gets wider.

I seek out a host so I can thrive.

I need a victim so I can survive.

A deer, a moose or even a bear.

I can burrow under the thickest hair.

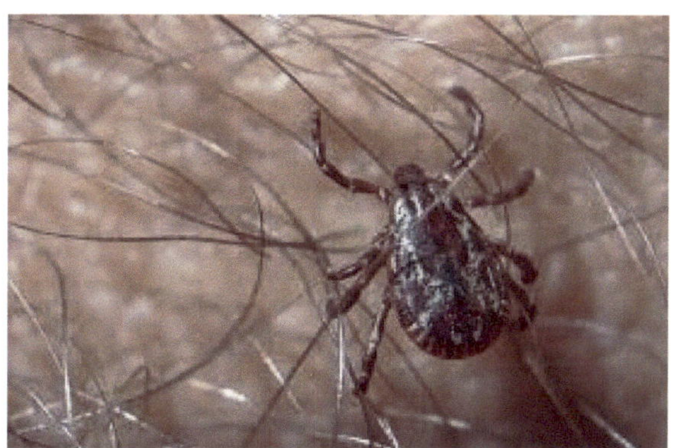

I'm sorry if you end up with Lyme disease.

Ticks are somewhat like our cousins, the fleas.

Mosquitoes, ticks, and other parasites.

Spread blood-borne diseases by way of their bites.

Don't be afraid, just use caution outdoors.

Protect yourself and your pet, it's one of your chores.

Nobody likes ticks I'm sorry to say.

I wish we could exist some other way.

THE LETTER 'U'

There are almost no insects which begin with a 'U'.

If you find a new one, here's what you do.

As an entomologist, you get to give it a name.

I hope it'll bring you fortune and fame.

Call it an uber-insect, which is German for super.

Please be a sport, please be a trooper.

This book is about insects from A to Z.

Please study them all and earn a degree.

THE VELVET MITE

Let me make one thing perfectly clear.

The velvet mite is one of the tiniest here.

The photo above is a close-up shot.

We're smaller than you probably thought.

We are harmless to humans, that's a fact.

We're cute and fuzzy, red velvet-backed.

Some say that I resemble a crab.

But you know how some people gab.

I'm really related to the arachnid or spider.

Four legs on each side, my body the divider.

Did you know that the red velvet mite,

Is known as a tiny parasite?

The insect we feed on is called the host.

A source of food when we need it the most.

After it rains, we sometimes appear.

Eager to eat or find a mate near.

I'll weave a silk path to lure a female.

I hope that she will follow my trail.

The study of mites is called acarology.

If it's news to you, there's no need for an apology.

Our bright red color is nature's warning sign.

Not to eat us, we don't taste at all fine.

Therefore, we have no predators.

Just other mites, our competitors.

THE **W**ASP

We vary in color from black to stripes yellow.

I'm not a particularly friendly fellow.

My thorax connected by a long, thin taper.

Our nest is constructed of layers of paper.

You can find thousands in just one nest.

One of the reasons we're considered a pest.

So keep your distance and avoid my sting.

Leave me alone, let me do my thing.

One drop of venom is all that it takes.

To make you realize all your mistakes.

You'll remember me by the welt on your skin.

And as a result of the pain that sets in.

Pirates with wings, intent on plunder.

If anything in our path should happen to blunder.

We have many hungry larvae to feed.

We need to find food if we're to succeed.

Should the winter turn extremely cold.

We'll die off before we grow old.

Don't you worry, we'll be back in the spring.

When the progenitor shall return and life it will bring.

THE LETTER 'X'

There are almost no insects which begin with an 'X'.

From the largest of beetles to the smallest of specks.

If you like insects, 'X' marks the spot.

We can be found wherever it's hot.

Some insects will freeze if it gets too cold.

We prefer warmth, if the truth is told.

Sometimes our eggs will remain dormant till spring.

We welcome the new hatch of bugs it will bring.

An insect's life is typically brief.

Each new generation is a welcome relief.

Large numbers are often called infestations.

Like locusts, cicadas and other relations.

Insects will come and insects will go.

We possess secrets nobody will know.

Some insects are good while others are cruel.

Survival of the fittest, that's nature's rule.

Study us hard, study us well.

For we have an interesting story to tell.

THE YELLOWJACKET

You know me, I am striped yellow and black.

I'd best warn you, if bothered, I'll attack.

With a hardened shell, like a suit of armor.

I scavenge for food, I'm no charmer.

And if you should happen to feel my sting.

You will soon realize the pain it will bring.

I'll have no sympathy if you should cry me some tears.

I might even frighten you, prey upon your fears.

You might think I'm nasty, you might think me mean.

I will spoil a picnic, I will cause a scene.

Some people wonder what purpose do I serve?

I'm one of God's creatures, you've got some nerve!

I'll tell you what, let's all agree.

I won't bother you, if you don't bother me.

THE ZEBRA CATERPILLAR

I'm long and plump with many legs in pairs.

I'm a curiosity, I draw lots of stares.

You'll find me crawling on vegetables green.

If I ruin your garden, you know where I've been.

I'm always hungry, is this the reason I'm fat?

On a healthy diet, imagine that!

Doctors say a person should eat vegetables to be thin.

Then why am I fat, is eating a sin?

And when it's time to transform, I'll spin a silky cover.

The change will surprise you, ask any butterfly lover.

Asleep in my cocoon, I will slim right down.

I will become light as a feather and fly around town.

EPILOGUE

As a young boy, I watched a frightening movie called "The Hellstrom Chronicle". The movie was a sensationalized, quasi-scientific, apocalyptic documentary which prophesied insects taking over the world. As much as I would like to deny that it had any effect on me, I still have a fear of certain insects. However, that fear has been assuaged by knowledge and admiration for insects in general. One can't help but admire their unique characteristics and adaptability. Secondly, knowing that there are insects which have a positive impact on the eradication of harmful pests and the production of food crops, flowering plants, and trees is reassuring. The plight of the honey bee is a particularly worthwhile cause of considerable magnitude. I have personally noticed marked reductions in populations of dragonflies, monarch butterflies, and honey bees. As a child, they were omnipresent during the spring and summer months and a source of entertainment and imagination. I hope that every child has a chance to interact with insects and the natural world. Our future depends on it.

Garry deGrood, Pomeroy, Washington